INDEX

Amazing Grace

John Newton (1725 - 1807)

1 John 1:9 If we confess our sins, He is faithful and just to forgive us our sins, and to cleanse us from all unrighteousness.

Blest Be the Tie that Binds

Hans G. Nageli

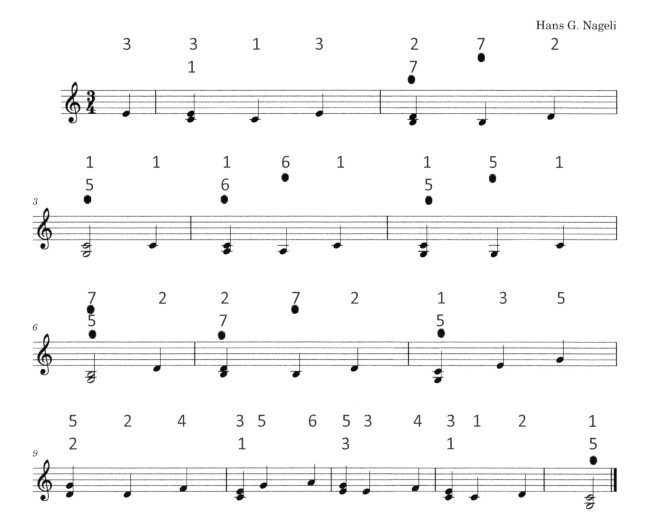

Hebrews 10:24-25 And let us consider one another to provoke unto love and to good works: Not forsaking the assembling of ourselves together, as the manner of some is; but exhorting one another: and so much the more, as ye see the day approaching.

This Is My Father's World

Franklin L. Sheppard

Genesis 2:1-3   Thus the heavens and the earth were finished, and all the host of them. And on the seventh day God ended His work which He had made; and He rested on the seventh day from all His work which He had made. And God blessed the seventh day, and sanctified it: because that in it He had rested from all His work which God created and made.

The Church has One Foundation

Samuel S. Wesley

*Ephesians 4:4-6 There is one body, and one Spirit,
even as ye are called in one hope of your calling; One
Lord, one faith, one baptism, One God and Father of
all, who is above all, and through all, and in you all.*

Come Thou Almighty King

Felice De Giardini

Revelation 17:14… for He is Lord of lords, and King of kings

O Worship the King

Johann Michael Haydn

1 Chronicles 16:29 …worship the LORD in the beauty of holiness.

Fairest Lord Jesus

Silesian Folk Tune

Malachi 4:2 But unto you that fear My name shall the Sun of righteousness arise with healing in His wings.

Jesus Loves Me

Anna Bartlett Warner (1827–1915)

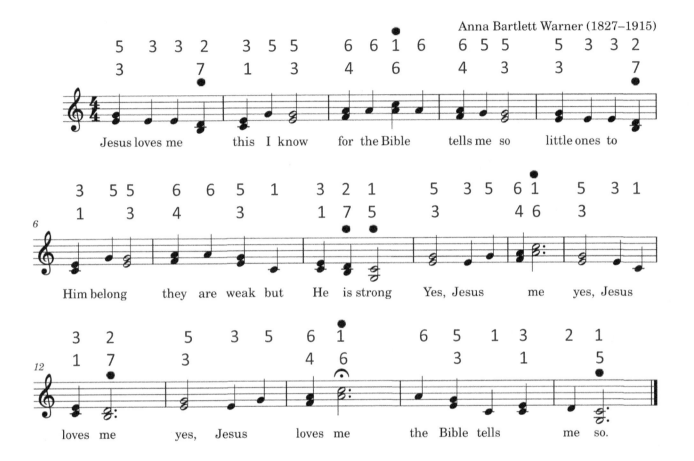

John 3:16-17   For God so loved the world, that He gave His only begotten Son, that whosoever believeth in Him should not perish, but have everlasting life. For God sent not His Son into the world to condemn the world; but that the world through Him might be saved.

Just as I Am

William B. Bradbury

Matthew 11:28-29   Come unto Me, all ye that labour and are heavy laden, and I will give you rest. Take My yoke upon you, and learn of Me; for I am meek and lowly in heart: and ye shall find rest unto your souls.

Sweet Hour of Prayer

William B. Bradbury

2 Chronicles 7:14   If My people, which are called by My name, shall humble themselves, and pray, and seek My face, and turn from their wicked ways; then will I hear from heaven, and will forgive their sin, and will heal their land.

Jesus Saves

William J. Kirkpatrick

*Romans 16:31   And they said, Believe on the Lord
Jesus Christ, and thou shalt be saved, and thy house.*

When I Survey the Wondrous Cross

Lowell Mason

Matthew 16:24 Then said Jesus unto his disciples,
If any man will come after Me, let him deny himself,
and take up his cross, and follow Me.

Jesus Keep Me Near the Cross

William H. Doane

1 Corinthians 2:2   For I determined not to know any thing among you, save Jesus Christ, and Him crucified.

Jesus the Very Thought of Thee

John B. Dykes

Isaiah 26:3-4   Thou wilt keep him in perfect peace, whose mind is stayed on Thee: because he trusteth in Thee.   Trust ye in the LORD for ever: for in the LORD JEHOVAH is everlasting strength:

In the Sweet By and By

Joseph P. Webster

Revelation 15:2 And I saw as it were a sea of glass mingled with fire: and them that had gotten the victory over the beast, and over his image, and over his mark, and over the number of his name, stand on the sea of glass, having the harps of God.

Beyond the Sunset

Blanche Kerr Brock

Mark 1:32   And at even, when the sun did set, they brought unto Him all that were diseased, and them that were possessed with devils.

Jesus Shall Reign

John Hatton

John 14:2-3   In My Father's house are many mansions: if it were not so, I would have told you. I go to prepare a place for you. And if I go and prepare a place for you, I will come again, and receive you unto Myself; that where I am, there ye may be also.

Shall We Gather at the River

Robert Lowry

Revelation 22:1 And he showed me a pure river of water of life, clear as crystal, proceeding out of the throne of God and of the Lamb.

Nearer My God to Thee

Lowell Mason

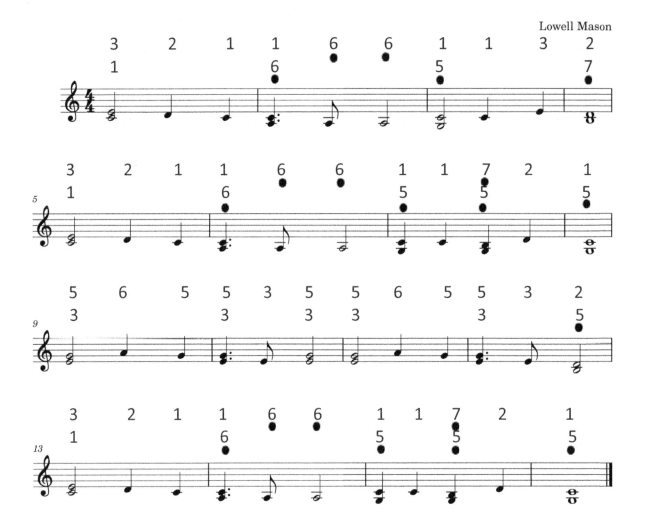

Colossians 1:26-27 Even the mystery which hath
been hid from ages and from generations, but now is
made manifest to his saints: To whom God would
make known what is the riches of the glory of this
mystery among the Gentiles; which is Christ in you,
the hope of glory:

My Faith Looks Up to Thee

Lowell Mason

Hebrews 11:6   But without faith it is impossible to please Him: for he that cometh to God must believe that He is, and that He is a rewarder of them that diligently seek Him.

Angels We have Heard on High

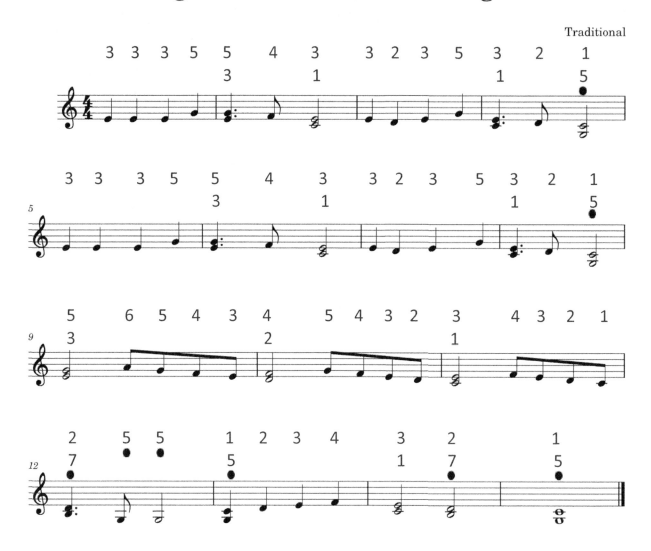

Luke 2:13-14   And suddenly there was with the angel a multitude of the heavenly host praising God, and saying, Glory to God in the highest, and on earth peace, good will toward men.

We Three Kings

John Henry Hopkins

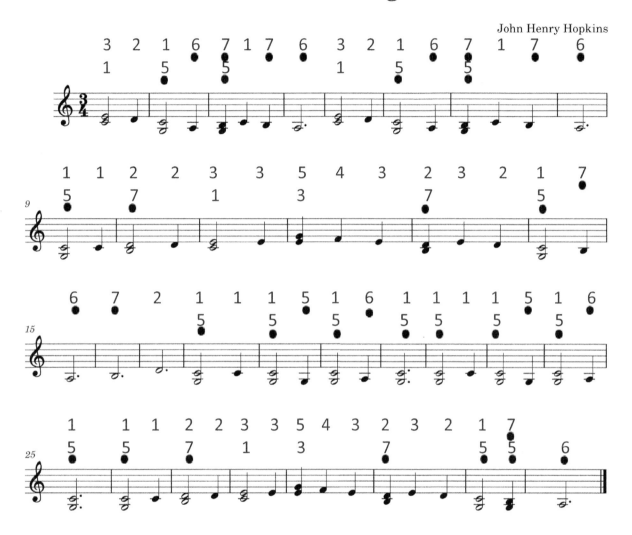

Matthew 2:1-2 Now when Jesus was born in Bethlehem of Judaea in the days of Herod the king, behold, there came wise men from the east to Jerusalem, Saying, Where is He that is born King of the Jews? For we have seen His star in the east, and are come to worship Him.

The First Noel

Luke 2:11-12   For unto you is born this day in the
city of David a Saviour, which is Christ the Lord.

Joy to the World

Luke 2:10-11   And the angel said unto them, Fear not: for, behold, I bring you good tidings of great joy, which shall be to all people. For unto you is born this day in the city of David a Saviour, which is Christ the Lord.

Holy Holy Holy

John B. Dykes

1 John 5:7   For there are three that bear record in
heaven, the Father, the Word, and the Holy Ghost:
and these three are one.

Joyful Joyful We Adore Thee

Ludwig Van Beethoven

Psalms 28:7   The LORD is my strength and my shield; my heart trusted in Him, and I am helped: therefore my heart greatly rejoiceth; and with my song will I praise Him.

O' Christmas Tree

German Traditional

Psalms 52:8 But I am like a green olive tree in the house of God: I trust in the mercy of God for ever and ever.

Praise Him, All Ye Little Children

Carey Bonner

Matthew 21:15...the children crying in the temple, and saying, Hosanna to the Son of David

Father Lead Me Day by Day

George C. Strattner

Psalms 23:3 ... He leadeth me in the paths of righteousness for His name's sake.

Amen

Traditional Folk Hymn

Matthew 6:10   Thy kingdom come. Thy will be done in earth, as it is in heaven.

Printed in Great Britain
by Amazon

44775541R00020